Pet Idol
Down Under

Helen Chapman

Ginn

Previously on Pet Idol Down Under

Welcome to *Pet Idol Down Under!* As we have seen so far on the show, Australia has many unusual animals that are found nowhere else on the PLANET! You have voted off four contestants already! (Go to pages 18 & 19 to meet these Pet Idol casualties.) Six contestants remain. Who will be the next to go?

> As you meet each contestant, write down and keep your answers to each **QUIZ** question. (Remember, the answers are in the book!) Let's get on with the show!

The Six Finalists

Sulphur Crested Cockatoo

Read about me first — I can live for over 60 years.

PAGES 6 TO 9

Frilled Neck Lizard

I am the reptile emblem of Australia — beat that!

PAGES 10 TO 13

Wombat

Who cares about age or emblems? I'm the world's largest burrowing animal.

PAGES 14 TO 17

Previously on Pet Idol Down Under

PAGES 18 TO 19

Sydney Funnel Web Spider

I'm the world's most dangerous spider — so there!

PAGES 20 TO 23

Saltwater Crocodile

Well I'm the biggest reptile in the world — AND I eat people!

PAGES 24 TO 27

Brown Snake

Listen to this! When I strike I have an almost 100% success rate!

PAGES 28 TO 31

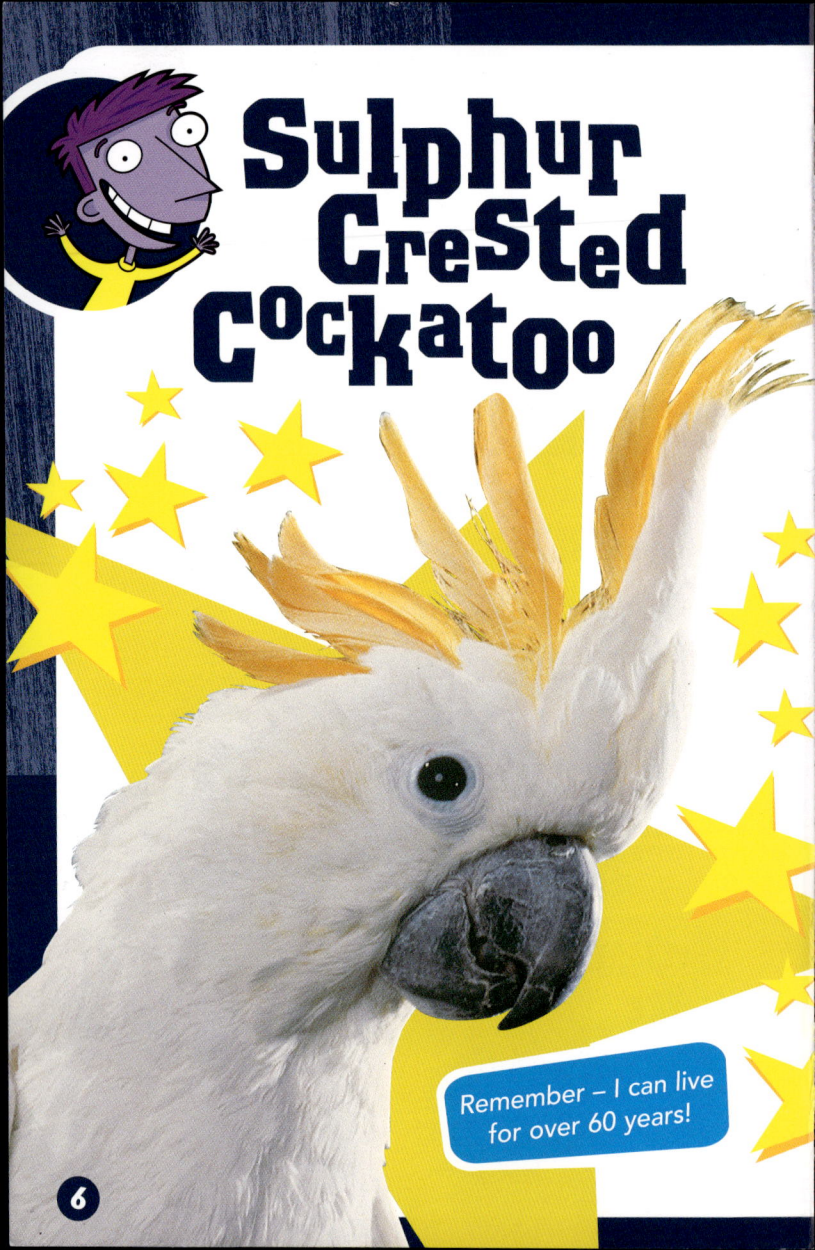

Sulphur Crested Cockatoo

Remember – I can live for over 60 years!

Vote for me!

I'm a beautiful, white parrot and I'd make a great Pet Idol. I'm friendly, love cuddles and bond with only one, special person. But watch out – we all need a hobby and mine just happens to be biting! I am very intelligent and need lots of branches to chew to keep me from getting bored. Okay, so I screech loudly, but wouldn't you if everyone you met asked "Polly, want a cracker?" … especially when your name is Bruce!

FLoCK FaCT

Cockatoos feed in large flocks. While most of the flock feeds on the ground, a few cockatoos perch in trees nearby. If danger approaches, these cockatoos will screech loudly and the whole flock flies away.

If that isn't enough to vote for me, listen to this! I'm clever and handsome and … I can fly! Yes, I have a series of fast wing beats. I also know a number of clever flap, flap, glide sequences. If you watch me fly, you'll see yellow feathers under my wings – just beautiful!

I can swoop really fast.

8 QUIZ The sulphur crested cockatoo likes to chew

Here are some more feathery facts to help you decide whether the sulphur crested cockatoo is your Pet Idol ...

Pet Idol Down Under Fact File

Sulphur Crested Cockatoo

Habitat	Most common in northern and eastern Australia and Tasmania. These cockatoos stay in the same area all year round.
Diet	Berries, seeds, nuts and roots (but they will also take handouts from humans).
Noise Level	High. But they can learn to mimic your voice!
Bad Habit	Destroying timber houses with their powerful beaks, chewing window frames and then moving onto decking for desserts. **What a pest!**

***** frames and ********.

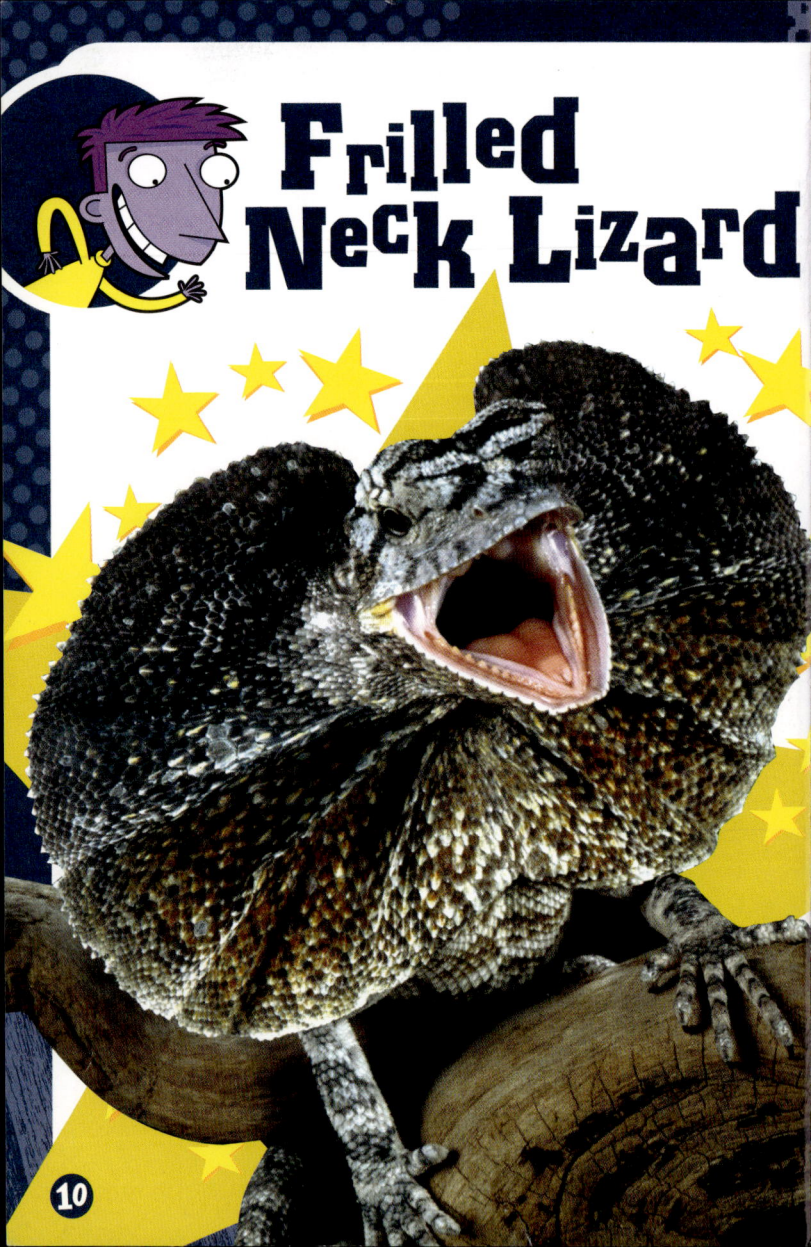

Frilled Neck Lizard

Vote for me!

When I open my mouth widely, my frill extends for 35 centimetres around my head. My frill doesn't just look good, it also helps me to control my body temperature – cool! I'd make the best Pet Idol ever. I spend 95 per cent of my time up in trees, so I don't need much looking after. At about 70 centimetres long you could even use me as a ruler to do your homework!

FRiLL FaCT

When the frilled neck lizard rests, its frill acts as a camouflage. It makes the lizard look like a branch or bark of a tree.

If all that is not enough to win your vote, just look at the many ways I can deal with danger. My self-defence plan is FRILLING!

1 Cringe & camouflage – I cringe on the ground and look like a fat, brown stick.

2 Bluff – I stick out my legs and open my mouth wide. Then I show my spectacular orange neck frill!

3 More bluffing – I hiss and jump towards the danger. I repeatedly lash my tail on the ground.

QUIZ The frill rests around the lizard's ****.

Here are some more frilly facts to help you decide whether the frilled neck lizard is your Pet Idol ...

Pet Idol Down Under Fact File

Frilled Neck Lizard

Habitat	Trees in eastern and northern Australia
Diet	Bugs, bugs and more bugs
Colour Co-ordination	The colour of the frilled neck lizard matches the land where it lives, making it a very colour co-ordinated creature. Males are more colourful than females!

4 Make sudden turn – I run off on back legs to the nearest tree. I climb until I'm out of reach of danger.

Wombat

I'm the world's largest burrowing animal!

Vote for me!

I love crashing through obstacles and my powerful legs let me run up to 40 kilometres per hour. I can grow to about 1.3 metres in length and can weigh up to 40 kilograms – so it makes it hard to stop if something gets in my way. What else makes me the perfect Pet Idol? I'm solid, so I'd make a great footstool. Oh, I'd particularly suit the lazy pet owner because I don't need any exercise.

FeMaLe FaCT

Female wombats have a pouch that opens backwards. This stops the dirt getting in when they dig.

Do you want to come over and see my burrow? It's a real vote winner! It is 30 metres long and up to 3.5 metres deep. Although I only just fit into my burrow, I can turn around in it. Did you know that my burrow is so big that it can be seen from space in satellite images?

My burrow has lots of entrances, side tunnels, and resting chambers, and they are all for me as I live alone.

QUIZ A wombat burrow has lots of ✼✼✼✼✼✼✼✼✼

Here are some more furry facts to help you decide whether the wombat is your Pet Idol ...

Pet Idol Down Under Fact File: Wombat

Nickname	Bulldozer of the bush
Habitat	Southern Australia. Wombats prefer slopes and dried creek banks, as these are better suited for digging burrows.
Diet	Grasses, herbs and roots (and wombats mostly feed at night).
Bad Habit	Marking out its territory by leaving smells and droppings. **What a stink!**

le tunnels and resting chambers.

Previously on Pet Idol Down Under

Tree Kangaroo

I can jump to the ground from 20 metres high without hurting myself! But I was too jumpy to win Pet Idol!

Blue-ringed Octopus

I'm the only venomous octopus in the world, so I was too dangerous to win Pet Idol. Sniff!

Platypus

I have the bill of a duck, the tail of a beaver and a furry body! But the viewers thought I was made up, so it was goodbye for me!

Koala

I am the only non-primate that has distinct and unique fingerprints. But I sleep for 20 hours a day, and when I woke up, I was out of the contest!

Sydney Funnel Web Spider

I'm the world's most dangerous spider!

20

Vote for me!

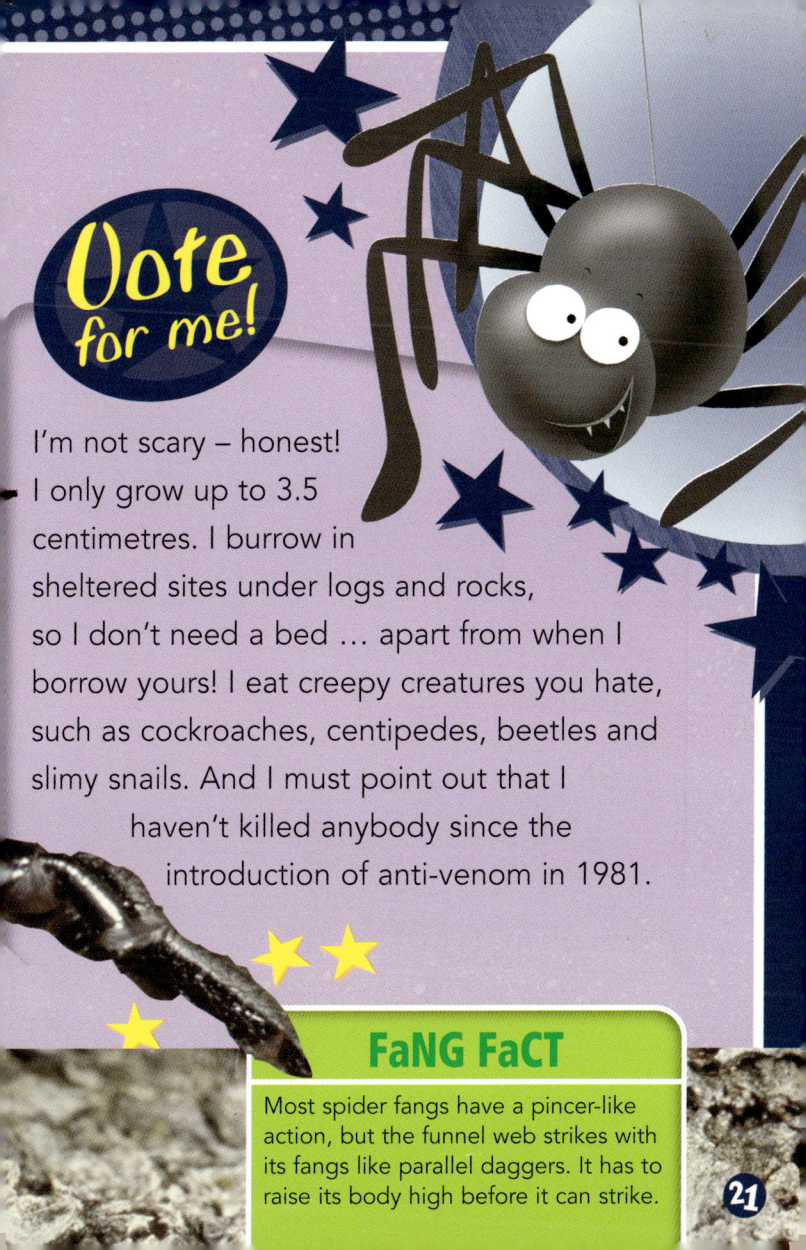

I'm not scary – honest! I only grow up to 3.5 centimetres. I burrow in sheltered sites under logs and rocks, so I don't need a bed ... apart from when I borrow yours! I eat creepy creatures you hate, such as cockroaches, centipedes, beetles and slimy snails. And I must point out that I haven't killed anybody since the introduction of anti-venom in 1981.

FaNG FaCT

Most spider fangs have a pincer-like action, but the funnel web strikes with its fangs like parallel daggers. It has to raise its body high before it can strike.

When voting, don't forget that I'm powerful and dangerous – what a deadly combination! I'm an all-action hero – try as you might to get rid of me, I keep on fighting back! No matter how much fly spray you use, you won't kill me. I can hold my breath for 72 hours straight! If I fall into your swimming pool, don't think that will be the end of me. I can trap air in hairs on my abdomen, and can survive for 30 hours underwater.

> Don't disturb me. I'll strike out and grip you with my front legs and stick my fangs into your skin over and over again.

22 QUIZ A funnel web's fangs are like parallel ******

Here are some more frightening facts to help you decide whether the Sydney funnel web spider is your Pet Idol ...

Pet Idol Down Under Fact File: Sydney Funnel Web Spider

Habitat	Sydney (but other funnel web spiders are found in southern and eastern Australia).
Diet	Bugs and small snakes. Relax – you are too big to eat!
Hobby	Female funnel web spiders enjoy spinning funnel-shaped webs that use trip wires to trap their prey.
Bad Habit	Hiding in houses. When it rains the funnel web spider crawls into places that will scare you the most, like your wardrobe, shoes or bed!

nd it can survive ✱✱✱✱✱✱✱✱✱✱ for 30 hours.

Saltwater Crocodile

I am the biggest reptile in the world!

Vote for me!

I am so strong I can overpower wild pigs, buffaloes and ... people like you! You won't see me – I'm a swift and silent mover. My eyes, ears and nostrils are on the same ridge on the top of my head. This way I can see, hear and breathe while almost totally under the water. Clever, huh? That's not all – my eyes have three pairs of eyelids, including a clear pair that protect my eyes when I'm underwater.

FaMe FaCT

I'm allowed one phone call, right?

Police in Western Australia had an unusual inmate in the station's lock-up ... Local rangers used the cell to hold a saltwater crocodile they'd found in the gardens of a nearby nursing home. The crazy croc had walked over a kilometre from a nearby creek!

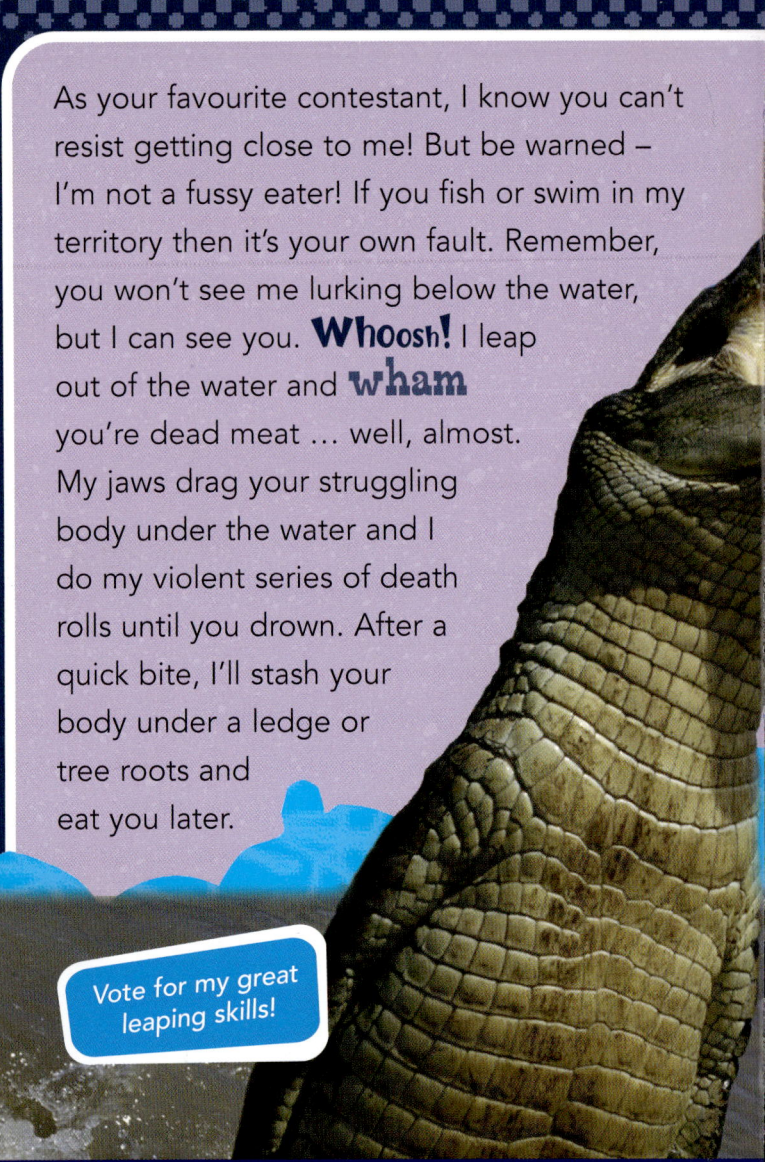

As your favourite contestant, I know you can't resist getting close to me! But be warned – I'm not a fussy eater! If you fish or swim in my territory then it's your own fault. Remember, you won't see me lurking below the water, but I can see you. **Whoosh!** I leap out of the water and **wham** you're dead meat … well, almost. My jaws drag your struggling body under the water and I do my violent series of death rolls until you drown. After a quick bite, I'll stash your body under a ledge or tree roots and eat you later.

Vote for my great leaping skills!

QUIZ A saltie can ********** wild pigs and buffalo

Here are some more ferocious facts to help you decide whether the saltwater crocodile is your Pet Idol ...

Pet Idol Down Under Fact File
Saltwater Crocodile

Nickname	Saltie
Habitat	Saltwater AND freshwater in northern Australia
Diet	Fish, birds, snakes and anything else it can get hold off (including YOU!)
Hobby	Showing off its speedy moves. It may look clumsy, but the saltie can out-run a horse over short distances. We're not even safe on land!

of these crocs took a trip from its creek to a ******* home!

Brown Snake

When I strike, I have an almost 100% success rate!

Vote for me!

I kill more people in Australia than any other snake! I coil my body into an amazing 'S' shape, raise myself off the ground and strike. I understand you just can't keep your hands off me! You claim to be looking for firewood when you pick me up, but you can't fool me. I may be long, brown and thick ... but I look nothing like a tree branch! It must be some kind of fatal attraction.

FRiGHTeNiNG FaCT

Snakes bite around 3000 Australians each year. And 95 per cent of bites are on the arms or lower legs of the snakes' victims.

I'm sure there must be some way we can live together. I know I'm very fierce, but if you stock up on anti-venom then I'm the perfect Pet Idol! There'll be a little pain and swelling when I bite, and you might get a headache, feel sick and start to throw up. But when the anti-venom kicks in, you'll be OK. The worse stages of snakebite – collapse, seizure, inability to move, and the deadly blood-clotting will never bother you – I promise!

Vote for me! Look, anti-venom just for you.

30 QUIZ The brown snake can ****** itself off the gro

Here are some more feverish facts to help you decide whether the brown snake is your Pet Idol ...

Pet Idol Down Under Fact File

Brown Snake

Habitat	In most parts of Australia, from fairly dry areas to wet bushlands. (There's no escape!)
Diet	Reptiles and small mammals, along with the occasional bird or frog
Bad Habit	Being extremely aggressive. Brown snakes strike again and again until they capture their prey. Then they wrap around the prey, and will not let go until the venom has worked.

trike!

Have you decided who is going to be your Pet Idol? It's a tough choice. Now, did you get the answers to all the questions? Juggle with the first letters of all the answers to find what all these Pet Idols have in common.

Bottles: entrances, daggers, underwater, neck, overpower, decking, nursing, window, raise

The first letters WDNEUONR become DOWN UNDER – our nickname for Australia and where all these Pet Idols live!

32